HANDBOOK
for the
EVOLVING
HEART

HANDBOOK
for the
EVOLVING HEART

through
Frank Coppieters, Ph.D.

CONFLU:X
PRESS

Marina del Rey, California

Author photograph by Harrison Merims.
Book design by Tania Baban.

ISBN: 0-9753559-9-6
Printed in Canada.

First Edition

CONFLU:X
PRESS

P. O. Box 12445, Marina del Rey, California 90295
www.confluxpress.com

*To my parents Georges Coppieters
and Jacqueline Coppieters-Ceriez
for their ongoing love and support.*

❋ *Acknowledgments*

I would like to express deep gratitude to all my
teachers and my special reverence for Mother Meera.
Each teacher has given me something precious and
has planted a seed in me.

In Reiki I honor especially Paul Mitchell, Phil
Morgan, Phyllis Furumoto, and all my Reiki students
who taught me to trust, to surrender, and then to
trust some more.

Gratitude to my mentors from the magical time
spent in theater research: Jerzy Grotowski, Ludwik
Flaszen, Saskia Noordhoek Hegt, Richard Schechner,
Rena Mirecka, Jacques Chwat, Ellen Stewart, Eugenio
Barba, Victoria Santa Cruz, and Luk De Bruyne.
Gratitude to the three spiritual giants whose love has
penetrated to my core: Jiddu Krishnamurti, Osho and
Chögyam Trungpa.

Gratitude to so many spiritual teachers whose
presence embodies the truth they share: Eckhart
Tolle, the Dalai Lama, Gangaji, Catherine Ingram,
Francis Lucille, U Silananda, Ammachi, Raymond
Diaz, Leslie Temple-Thurston, and Douglas and
Catherine Harding.

Gratitude to *A Course in Miracles*, the book that
transformed all my relationships.

Gratitude to my life-long shamanic teacher
Joska Soos whose example, encouragement, and art

has helped to make the dimensions beyond the known a lived reality.

Gratitude to Roland Barthes, the French semiotician, who was the academic teacher from whose seminars I have learned the most.

Gratitude to a host of teachers whom I have never met in the body and yet are so close to my heart: Ramana Maharshi, St.Germain, Nityananda, Meher Baba, Sri Aurobindo, Sweet Mother, Babaji, Nisargadatta Maharaj, Ramakrishna, and Wolter Keers.

Gratitude to so many friends who have sat in meditation with me and encouraged me to channel the wisdom they felt was there. Your enthusiasm and responses have kept me going: Joe Keeney, Cynthia Alvarado, Neal Nemhauser, Marilyn Powers, Fred Bryson, Dagmar Lünser, Nancy Simmons, Aurelia Adams, Ann Wall Frank, Barbara Jolley, Mike Iannantuano, Arlene Holmes, Bob and Jodi Eaton, Anna DeMers, Bob White, Joost Vanhove, Els Van Hoogenbemt, Rita Helsen, Anne Solseng, Paul and Margie Carlson, Marie-Gabrielle Cuvelier, Mega McGrew, Tommy and Leslie Harris, Julie Zehetbauer, Victoria Elisabeth Field, Dianne Geldon, Peggy Hoyt, Cheryl Beam, and Hilda and Lionel Pinn. This list goes on and on. As I sit I often feel you sitting around me.

Gratitude to Carla Riedel who became such a great companion as the guidance was being shaped into a book. Your advice, your keen sense of rhythm, your receptive heart and vision made this final process into a dream come true.

Gratitude to my dear friend Simone D'Aubigné, whose mandalas reflect what these words attempt. She dedicates her mandalas to her husband John Robert LeBow for all his loving support.

Gratitude to my most beloved wife Kathy Melcher. You inspire me every single day to be the best I can be. Your love makes this stay on earth such a pleasant and rewarding adventure. Words fail to thank you.

Finally, gratitude to Jim Natal and Tania Baban of Conflu:x Press for taking their time to meet me, encourage me, and for all their professional, creative, and artistic input.

✸ *Table of Contents*

✸ *Genesis of the Inspired Guidance*

Around age four I had a near death experience. Our family doctor had become sufficiently worried about my symptoms (extreme dehydration and diarrhea, probably as a result of anaphylactic shock) to rush me to the hospital where for a day or two I hovered between the dimensions. This was in 1954 in Belgium where I grew up and lived until I was thirty-five.

When I go back to this early incident I can only pull up a few scattered memories and feelings such as the loving concern of my parents who were terribly distraught about the prospect of losing me. I know that both of my grandmothers, and one of them a devotee of Mother Mary, were praying very hard for me, and I could sense the presence of a divine form. The most remarkable thing was that I, the sick little boy, knew something beyond a doubt that the grown-ups didn't seem to: I was not going to leave this earth plane, at least not as yet and not for a long time to come. I did not question this knowing. There was both a comfort in it and a quiet strength and above all a certain clarity that did not seem to come from me personally and yet was somehow available, at least during these dramatic circumstances.

The rest of my childhood was relatively uneventful except for recurring nightmares in which I would try to solve the mystery of time. In my dreams it felt like I had to go back to before time began and, each time I got close to it, a terrible fear came over me and I would scream. My

Dad would then come, take me to the bathroom and sponge off my face with cold water. It would usually take me about half an hour to be back in regular consciousness. By the time I reached the age of seven or eight those dreams stopped. When I was ten years old I had a distinctive past life memory. It came to me while I was acting in a play in which I was both a Jewish boy and the son of a German officer. A couple of times in the play the name of Yahweh (God of the Hebrews) was mentioned. I had no idea what this meant but could not stop repeating this to myself, as if the word was some sort of mantra.

I had been raised Catholic, as was everybody else at that time in Belgium, though not too strict, and at the age of twelve I had another glimpse of what felt like a past life experience on the day of my confirmation (a rite conferring the gift of the Holy Spirit). The whole day, in the midst of the festivities, I had fleeting memories of a childhood as a Jewish girl. Two years later, after thinking for quite awhile about God and religion, I announced to my mother that I would not go to church anymore since it did not feel authentic to me. In some ways this was my first spiritually conscious decision. It would take me about twenty years to become fully comfortable and intrigued again with the more esoteric mystery teachings of the Christian tradition.

During my early twenties and throughout my thirties I became absolutely obsessed with the spiritual search. I tried to reconnect with a larger dimension that I seemed to have lost mostly by the very rigorous academic and mental training that I had taken upon myself. I started to commit myself to daily meditations, became a participant in innumerable workshops, traveled to be in the company of shamans and awakened teachers. In the midst of all this spiritual searching, I had quite a variety of mystical and awakening experiences.

I remember a funny event that happened to me in those days. The renowned Sufi order-of-the-whirling-dervishes from Koina in Turkey were coming to Belgium for a performance. I was very excited to have an opportunity to see them and my younger brother had arranged for tickets for this event for a small group of us. When we arrived at the performance hall, it turned out that we were one ticket short and the performance was sold out. For some reason I was the one who ended up without a ticket. My younger brother thought of a scheme: he would go in first and then come back to go to the restroom and then get me in with his ticket. So we did. The seats were numbered though. I felt quite calm even though in general my personality really does not want to create any difficulties for others or for myself. I sat down in the theater waiting for how this was going to turn out and did not really have a plan in my mind. Pretty soon an usherette came with a gentleman who wanted to have my seat. To my great surprise I heard myself say (in a gentle voice but also with a quiet authority in it): "But I am Dr. Coppieters". I found it strange that I used my academic title which I never used in public at all. Very strangely the usherette took this to mean (I guess) that I was a medical doctor and that somehow I was sitting there in case some accident would happen with these whirling dervishes. She apologized to me and arranged for a loose chair to be brought and created an extra, very good seating for the gentleman on whose place I was sitting. I was absolutely flabbergasted. Something had taken place here where I had been a willing witness, an instrument of a force beyond my little will, and had come up with a perfect solution working out for everybody. It is true that there had been a deep longing in my heart to see the dervishes perform their sacred ritual. Apparently, Kidhr, the mysterious guide of the Sufis had come as a response to my longing and had spoken through me. The friends in my party, who knew me quite well, had a good laugh over this and were equally startled since all of this was quite out of character for me.

For many years I worked on the campus of the University of Antwerp in Belgium. My initial status was assistant professor and I was charged with courses on literary theory, drama, and non-verbal communication. In the seventies this was a new and quite liberal college and there were only graduate students in our program. After a couple of years of being on campus I established the Center for Experimental Theater and it became my responsibility to invite artists from all over the world to teach workshops and bring performances. With a fairly limited budget we were able to offer some of the best avant-garde theater available in those days. I was personally deeply affected by the work of the famous Polish theater director Jerzy Grotowski and his collaborators. They were masters much disciplined in making the body into a supple instrument for creative impulses. I was not an actor but learned from them the art of improvisation.

I found it quite exciting to explore the body-mind connection within an academic context. I was able to study with some brilliant language philosophers in Paris, great psychologists in Oxford, and go to many cutting edge conferences. The academic freedom in my university encouraged creativity and nobody had any objections when I took the initiative to introduce students to various forms of meditation. But spirit had something else in mind. After I had successfully presented the oral defense of my Ph.D. dissertation entitled "Towards a Performance Theory of Environmental Theater" I was awarded tenure in my department. Still, there was a growing sense that all this was not really my life's work. Sometimes I would meditate for many hours in the little cottage that I rented just opposite the campus. Then I would walk to my office and feel in my gut that academia was no longer the world I belonged to. After thirteen years I decided to quit and go to the States to fully devote myself to spiritual matters. I was then thirty-five years old. Some of my colleagues understood, some thought I was making a big mistake. Some of my family members were quite worried about me. I felt very excited about where the journey would lead me. The last seminar I offered to my students had as a textbook *Zen Mind, Beginner's Mind* by the Japanese Zen meditation master Shunryu Suzuki (1905-1971). The spontaneous talks to his American students are collected in this beautiful classic. In many ways this book, and my last course, already contained my own future.

I had traveled many times to the States mostly in connection with my work and had received a grant to do post-doctoral research at New York University where I had studied for about a year. In 1984, I met Kathy, my future (American) wife, who shared most of my spiritual endeavors and fully supported my journey into my new homeland. Of course I suffered from culture shock but there was also a deep sense of joy about receiving a chance

to reinvent myself and to start my life from scratch. Here
I was also following and experiencing the myth and the
reality of the American dream. In 1986, I became a licensed
massage therapist and made sandwiches in a restaurant
for awhile to earn a living. Continuing to listen to inner
promptings, I worked as a massage therapist in a beauty
salon and for several chiropractors. I became a Reiki Master
and soon after that I was very busy as an energy worker and
spiritual counselor. I was also teaching again, frequently in
Europe and the U.S.

Every so often a spontaneous out of body experience
would occur and open a door into a realm of sacred love
that interpenetrated ordinary reality. Sometimes these states
were triggered by visits to special places (churches in
Europe, healing temples in Egypt); sometimes during
rebirthing sessions or receiving bodywork, but also sometimes while vacationing with Kathy and simply relaxing. One
other event stands out: in 1991 a reputable trance medium
in London predicted that one day I would channel teachings
that would be useful for many people around me. The
responsibility and excitement of this potential mission fright-
ened and attracted me at the same time. But it was true that
I felt a growing ability to go in and out of a heightened sense
of perception and a deepening ability to capture wisdom
from the world of spirit. As I did professional healing
sessions, guides from this world would be solidly present,
providing me with their support.

By this time I had benefited enormously from being in
the presence of three formidable present-day teachers. Two
were from India: Jiddu Krishnamurti (1895-1986) and Osho
(1931-1990), and one was from Tibet: Chögyam Trungpa

(1940-1987). Their teachings were quite different but touched my heart each in their own way, and for this I will always be grateful. I heeded Krishnamurti's message that there is no path to truth and that the pitfalls of following a guru blindly can deny one's own inner light. From Osho I learned the art of meditating and the notion that spirituality and materialism do not have to be mutually exclusive. Trungpa taught me about silencing the mind and the seductiveness of spiritual materialism.

Many teachers whom I had never met became constant companions in my work and meditations. Once, while visiting a shrine of the legendary Indian yogi Bhagavan Nityananda (d.1961) a peculiar light entered me that would profoundly affect my healing work. The strongest connection of all, one that would never fade in or out, is with the great Indian saint Ramana Maharshi (1879-1950). Once, while teaching a Reiki class in London in the Ramana Maharshi Center, his energy poured into my heart. Later, his so-called non-dual teachings would make a bridge from my mind to my heart. I especially loved his succinct and paradoxical formulation:

> *The world is illusory;*
> *Brahman (God) alone is real;*
> *Brahman is the world.*

I also read thousands of pages of the work of Sri Aurobindo (1872-1950) and Mirra Alfassa (the Mother, or Sweet Mother) (1878-1973), two great yogis who had dedicated their whole lives to an "integral yoga." In Aurobindo's integral yoga "tantra" refers to the union of the yoga practitioner with "shakti," the energy of the Divine Mother, in order to effect a transformation of material life.

Even though I had never met Aurobindo or Sweet Mother on the physical plane, both of them became intimate guides. The story of the last years of Mother's life fully engaged in a yoga of physical transformation fascinated me more than anything. Then, in 1993, I became aware that there was a young Indian woman in Germany called Mother Meera. She was considered one of several incarnations of the Divine Mother. I visited her whenever I could be back in Europe and typically would be very happy and extremely grateful in her company. After having been mostly with male teachers it was now the sacred feminine that gave me deep nourishment. This energy struck me as being so loving, soft, protective, patient, all accepting and, at the same time, tremendously powerful in its ability to transform. I also loved that this work took place in utter and deep silence. The contact with this Divine Mother energy prepared me for my next step.

In the summer of 2000 my wife and I vacationed in the magical Mount Shasta area in Northern California. We had invited two good friends of ours to join us for a week. While meditating with them they solicited me to let some guidance come through. I was happy to oblige and very soon a new tradition was born. Back at home in Portland, Oregon, more people started to come to sit together in meditation. Shortly after the events of 9/11 I decided to start recording the words as they came through and send them out over email in an attempt to share light in a world that suddenly seemed darker than before.

The guidance turned out to be non-sectarian and not affiliated with any particular philosophy or religion. It came from many sources of inspiration. It reflects my own interests and comes in easy, often poetic words. I remain fully conscious during these channelings, my voice sometimes changes a little bit and the atmosphere in the room is often charged with light and a palpable, rejuvenating silence. The words well up straight out of the heart, not only my heart but also the heart of the people meditating with me and, one could say, from the collective heart. Similarly the "you" that is spoken to is not just the audience, but also "myself" and during the rest of the day or weeks I find it most useful to remind myself often of the guidance.

To my initial surprise people would very often share these passages with friends and collect them one by one in big binders. Many reports came to me from strangers who felt this guidance spoke directly to them. Somebody started making "holy cards" with them, some would read a page before sitting down to meditate, others would take two lines that spoke to them and use them throughout the day. Every so often I would hear about a yoga or Tai Chi teacher reading these texts aloud during their classes.

Now the time has come to share some of these with you...

Coming into Guidance

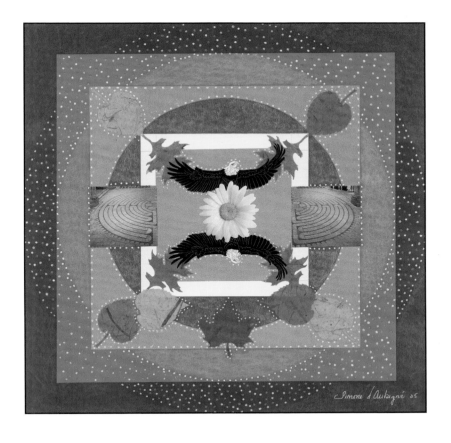

i.

The great unknown is preparing you
to step beyond yourself into the mystery of Divine Love.
You are being asked to let go of that which is not love.
Let go of what no longer serves the highest good.

Ask "What is the highest good?" and guidance will show you.
Guidance comes from Source
which, in your heart, you have never left.

You cannot leave what you are.
Such is Divine Law.
Divine Law has been established beyond time
and can be accessed in the Eternal Now.

To live in the Eternal Now is what you came here to do.
Living in the Eternal Now allows you
to heal and remember who you truly are.

ii.

Banish all thoughts from your mind for awhile
and allow the voice of guidance to come to you.

This voice is never harsh but speaks with wisdom
and authority to remind you of your true nature.

The knowledge it shares already belongs to you.
How else would you resonate with it?

Only the heart can hear these messages and respond to them.
Yet sometimes an angel drops the message
        from the heart into the mind.

How sweet this conversation between you and your true self.
It is the lover calling the beloved.

iii.

The world cannot touch your sovereign self.
This is where your inner teacher resides and communes
with the highest information you are now able to receive.
The world is still a battleground, but more and more of you
know that this cannot possibly be the way.
The way is to contact the peace within, especially when fear
and disturbance have come to visit you.
Your willingness to do this is all that is asked of you.

iv.

The times are critical and yet your task remains the same.
Listen to higher guidance steeped in love for all and everything.

There are many here to support you.
Together you are the emissaries of transformation.

Sweet Mother has planted a flower in your heart.
Its fragrance shall remind you of who *you* are.

v.

Wherever you are there is only one truth.
It is your teacher.

Your life has been guided all along.
Trust this is so even today.

In these critical times, holding peace in your heart
is the essence of being a spiritual warrior.

Rest in the silence between your thoughts;
habit is then replaced by wonder.

Only love matters.
To know this is the end of your search.

Do not wait for the miracle,
for it is right here.

vi.

It is your inner teacher who leads you to an outer one.
In the joy of this recognition there is no more separation.
Both disappear as they bow respectfully to each other.

vii.

A shiny pearl of wisdom
is nestled in your heart center.
In silent communion it whispers
guidance to you.
Trust...and listen to *this*.

I.
Awareness and Awakening

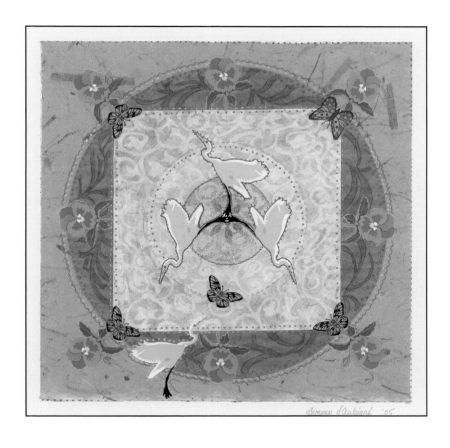

Acknowledge how far you have come
and remain open to even greater blessings.

It is only a flawed perception that prevents you
from seeing yourself as perfection.

Many lifetimes of searching have brought you to this moment.
Now is the time to wake up.

There is a place in you where all is always well.
It is the place of the witness.

The witness is already awakened consciousness
and from its vantage point every single event
can either trigger or stabilize your awakening.

Awakening occurs as the heart opens
and you are able to see yourself
in a compassionate and impersonal way.

Witnessing is not an activity.
It is simply the awareness that you *are* the witness.
You are not invested in how things turn out
because the witness just *is*.
Unshakable peace results from this position.
You can be active in the world from this place,
but now the world moves in you, not you in the world.

Know that you are an anchor for many around you.
Let this not be a burden, let this be your strength.

As you abide steadily in the one and only eternal Self
you are connected to all that is:
the dance of the rain,
the movement of the earth and stars,
the dimensions beyond time and space.

Even if your life circumstance today is challenging
do not shut down your heart center.
Let the rays of hope and love shine through it.

Becoming aware of awareness is an ongoing process
that stabilizes you forever in the Now.
Remember, awakening occurs in a split second.

In deep sleep the world completely disappears.
In deep meditation even the meditator is no longer there.
In life the world reappears but it is not your identity.

These are guidelines for awakening.

The mind sees the Now as dull and empty.
For the heart it is real and full and deeply satisfying.

When you stay present with what arises
you are led upstream until you reunite with Source.

The purpose of awakening is to dispel the illusion of separation.
Nothing else is holding back the evolution of your planet.

•

Life is a string of pearls
and this moment is always the most precious one.
Awakening will always be now or never.

Consciousness is eternal
and evolves through many forms.
The mystery of your form
can only be grasped through introspection.

In meditation you experience that
simply being is much superior to thinking.
Apply this now wherever you go.

There is no difference between the love
that created you and the love that you are.

To know this and to live in this knowing
is the glorious path of awakening.

Rest now, for all your efforts have brought you here.
To go beyond, only grace can take you.

You are unobstructed awareness
forever free – even now.
Allow the deep connection to all that is
and your unique expression will flow.
You are *always* part of the divine whole.

Is there any validity in the belief
that full awakening would not be available
to you right now, in this moment?
Check for yourself.

Who is the one holding this belief?
Check for yourself.

Who is the one watching this belief in action?
Check for yourself.

The one who is watching is limitless
and has been watching since the beginning of time.

This watching is as natural
as a gentle morning rain —
no effort, no intention.

Every single raindrop reaches its final destiny,
so why do you think you will not?

Be thankful for what you have but mostly for what you are —
radiant awareness...

When going through a transition
give yourself permission to reinvent yourself.
Choose freedom, choose creativity,
and especially choose to be your authentic self.

In the center of the storm
there is an immense quiet.
Find that place within yourself
and live your life from it —
undisturbed, efficient, at peace.

Awareness is already fully within you.
Can you become aware of this awareness?
It may sound tricky, yet it is simple.

There are many seekers galvanizing one another
into higher consciousness, like a swarm of bees
buzzing each other into ecstasy.

Hold a steady field of loving presence.
It is your greatest contribution on this earthly plane.

Even now you make a difference —
simply by sharing your own essence.

Ground yourself in witnessing presence.
This is the only action taking place in meditation.

Your awareness is then unobstructed and centered;
like that of the mountains, the trees, the rivers,
at ease with itself and the world.

50

When you balance doing and non-doing, you walk
the golden middle path.

A higher teaching can be received through any life circumstance.
Everything you experience helps to connect you with truth.

Clarity of vision washes away years of misunderstanding
all at once.

All over the planet the field of awakening consciousness
is strengthening.
Tap into it frequently for your own benefit.

Now is the time to set your boundaries with compassion for
yourself and others.

No lesson is learned well
until you share it with others—
joyfully.

Your true essence will always thrive beyond time and space.
When you are grounded in this perspective
you care tremendously about the here and now.

Revelation takes place when you allow yourself to disappear
in the gap between two thoughts,
the gap between two breaths
and the gap between dimensions.

By letting go of control existence itself
will lead you to your next level of awareness.

Awakening is seeing through the illusion of the world
and blessing it with your clarity.

The path is not difficult to find.
It is wherever you have chosen to show up
as the love that you are.

Your beautiful presence makes a world of difference.

At the end of time only one event will stand out...
your ability to see yourself as love.

Your true nature is vaster than the sky.
It has no beginning, no end, and nothing can contain it.
It touches everything with love.
May this great expansion carry you through the day.
You are not the clouds. You are beyond the sky.
You are timeless love. You are All that Is.

Surrender to love. This is one decision you will never regret. With love as your teacher life flows in unexpected ways and brings you to the home where Divine Mother and Divine Father hold you in a tender embrace.

Once you know that love exists even on earth, and that you belong to it, a path of initiation opens up and all illusions are seen for what they are. You do not walk this path alone. Friends, teachers, and even some difficult people, share this journey with you. Steeped in unity consciousness you can relax deeply, knowing that the world is not so real as compared to the reign of love and that this love is eternal and invincible.

Love's temple stands untouched in the midst of lies, corruption, and injustice. Here you find strength to move about in a world hungry for harmony. Remember, the Bodhisattvas are returning to the world until the light is shared by all. When these words touch your mind or your heart *you* are surrendering to the flow of love. Kuan Yin – Bodhisattva of Compassion – Avatar of the Age is pouring her essence into you, now, and into the world so all may live in decency, without poverty, in love, and in peace.

You are the light that you have been looking for!
Look within! This light is beyond words. It is even
        beyond silence.
It is all pervading and very concentrated in the heart.
As the universal light expands so do you.
Your heart is big enough to bless the whole world!

True meditation lies beyond the mind. It descends on you and you become pure presence. As you invite this presence wherever you are, life becomes one extended meditation. Love without preference is the center of such a presence, and such a love is not of this world yet blesses and transforms all that is. Wrap yourself in this blanket of love.

Surrender the notion that you are a limited entity
and immediately your mediation will propel you
beyond the mind into the heart of the universe.

Here bliss and creation and peace
cannot be disturbed by worldly events.

Meditation frees your mind from obsession
so you may rest into the one subject that is *always* you.
Do not think about it. Simply let it happen...

Any gap between two thoughts will do for freedom to come and find you.

Can you conceive of yourself as vast energy
not yet touched by culture or concepts?
Here all is possible...for without attachments
to concepts you are free. In freedom you are open.

Love has nothing to prove and knows itself as the ultimate of what is. When love is your foundation the world ceases to be a frightening place. As you experience this as truth you will no longer search for substitutes and will accept yourself and everyone else. It is a most positive thing to live with only love as your ally, for once in awhile even the world, with all its dark and gloom, will light up and let you in.

Try to imagine the eagerness
with which you leapt into incarnation.
Bring that freshness to your day.

It is time for seekers of truth to unite and proclaim
celebration as the highest form of civilization.
The Divine invites you to send messages of love all over
        the earth.

Hold everyone in your heart as a most tender flower now.
People need love, the planet needs love, and so do you.
Gathered in the name of love, the miracle of transformation
        takes place.

If something oppresses you, give it to love.
Love is all accepting. Love cannot hold on. Love flows freely.
What a simple formula!

Here is a message of love:

Your thoughts are creating the world. What would happen if
you knew that you are divine perfection as you are right now,
this moment?
Experiment with this perception. No longer will you look for
approval or outside validation. You will rest in your true self
where all is well.

Know this...Love is what you are. What a wondrous mantra
to speak:
*I am love...I am love...*until all the cells of your body repeat
this in unison and you relax completely because you know
this is so. *I am love...I am love...*
This you say to yourself.

*You are love...You are love...*This you say to those you encounter.
Then a brilliant sun will awaken your mind, open your heart,
and change the world.

The whole cosmos hears you and responds to you...
There is so much hope because of your deep yearning to open
to love.

There are many sacred places on and beyond this planet.
In your meditation and your dream time
allow yourself to be transported to these sanctuaries of light.

Imagine you are sitting in the middle of a magnificent cathedral.
Through each of the stained glass windows the light
filters through your chakras and celestial music sings you
back into harmony.

What you have gained in so many lives is now being synthesized
so that you may step joyfully into the new paradigm. Many have
come forward to guide you; some in form and some hardly
visible. Your heart has prepared for this ascension.

Those who love you have promised to stand by you until your
purpose has been fulfilled. Whenever you need to, reenter
the cathedral of light. This is the renewal for which you have
been thirsting.

In a precarious world nothing can prevent
your consciousness from touching all things
    with peace and love.

Peace is who you are. Allow this to be your mantra today
and let it resound all over the planet as hope and joy
    and affirmation.

•
74
•

Many of your relations are reconfigurations from past lives. Now all of you have come to serve the common purpose of your great transformation.

Know you are loved and that your suffering is
a misunderstanding.
Be with these words until they become your reality.

From the awakened perspective, no event in life is without merit or opportunity. What matters is your response to it. In spite of all past programming, you can still claim full freedom. The freedom to be who you truly are is priceless and does not rely on any outward situation. What love calls forth from you will change any challenging experience into a treasured teaching.

There is no separation between you and the divine impulse.
You are it!

For now say *no* to your thoughts.
Say *yes* to presence and to love.
Say *yes* to fully embracing your Buddha nature.
A subtle relaxation in the body occurs, and in the mind too.
You may feel teachers and guides surrounding you.
Deeper and deeper into the majesty of your being you go.
Awakening is happening. Nothing stands in the way.
Love responds to love. This is Cosmic Law.
To live this way invites the miracle.

Pure love has a very high vibration...
It changes you as you take it in...
It opens you as you send it out...

True love is not blind, yet forgives everything
in one instant of wisdom in action.

You are so fortunate that you have come to serve.
Nothing else can make you happy.

Who is the one who already knows all this? It is the one
who never leaves you, the one who guides you home to the heart.

Love's only requirement of you is this...
Be fully present to this moment.

When you come home to yourself others can find themselves in you.

At the center of your mind there is peace.
It was born at the time of your creation.
Ask an enlightened being to take you there
so you can rest and feel God's love for you.

You came here to see divine love in all forms—
        even the confused ones.
It is through your seeing that even they are transformed.

As you see sameness rather than differences
        you are unified.

Then a force gathers in you that has intelligence,
one that knows how to act within the world.

Share what you are—
        You are light.
        You are joy!

A few moments in deep silence
and all your cells rearrange themselves
into a new harmony.

As you sit the world flows through you.

The limiting beliefs you have carried about yourself
no longer serve you. Discard them right now so you can
be on equal footing with the Divine and celebrate each
other. Remember, love is your natural state. You have heard
this message many times before and now *you* have come
as the messenger.

Know this...When you feel desperate
and have lost all perspective you are still the Beloved.

Know this...Without you this world loses value,
for you are the shining face of the Divine.

What legacy will *you* leave behind?
Let it be love and only love,
for love is what you are.
To know this and live in this way
is your only goal and your current practice.
Welcome to such a splendid life!

Your heart knows this much...
No matter what you think about yourself,
you *are* the Beloved.

III.
Meditation

Meditation and service are the pillars
of a life dedicated to the Divine.

In the practice of sitting silently — doing nothing —
transformation takes place by itself.

When all seeking ceases
you and the Divine are One.

Just notice…When the mind intrudes upon
            the present moment, yield to it.
After all, this too is a natural phenomenon occurring
            in the now.

Just notice…When the mind leaves the present
            moment alone,
it is strong and brilliant and full of awakening potential.

There is no effort in meditation...
When the mind is busy welcome this...
When the mind is silent cherish this...

What luxury it is to not dwell on thoughts and to feel your own oneness with the vast love and intelligence that is creating you moment-by-moment. Relax into this place...rest and rejuvenate. Awake and alert, free from fears and free from worries. To be in the Now, even for a few split seconds, allows your meditation to shift into a radical practice of transformation.

Meditation is the time you choose
to be with your guides and teachers.
In this time they will purify your crown chakra
and in the silence they will answer all your questions.
Now your mind can rest in pure awareness.

Between thoughts, slip away and don't come back.
The world will reappear when you need it.

During deep meditation dark is transformed into light.
This alchemy is an ongoing mystery.

Ask the wind to open your chakras until each one has become a beautiful mandala of peace and happiness. Absorb the spiritual light through the crown chakra and let it circulate through the heart. Ground it in the sacrum and the feet. In this way, meditation becomes a reconnection with your true nature which is *always* radiance. To know yourself as this radiance is to undo all conditioning and reclaim your freedom.

The light of meditation opens new pathways in the brain.
As you sit, silently welcoming the divine dimension,
many unseen presences come to assist you.
When you taste the transcendent,
you are no longer the prisoner of time and space.

Life is sacred.
All of life — the animate and the inanimate.
Every breath, every pulse of the heart.

In meditation merge with the Sacred.
For your sake — for life's sake.

The benediction of the Sacred descends through
your reverence and appreciation...your silence.

And though the world is in shambles, you need not be.
Build your own alliance with what is true...
for that which is beautiful and worth living...

Just for now forget about unraveling your troubles and entanglements. Simply establish yourself in the shining presence of your own true nature through your daily meditation. Here you are self sufficient, and here lies the answer to all your sadness. Here is peace...

Every meditation is a new invitation
to explore your *self* as if for the very first time.

Stop the movement of thought towards the past and the future
and sit in the loving embrace of this moment.

How miraculous...the dimension of the Now is not static!
It brings you deeper and deeper into the core of your own being.

As you enter your own true self give rise to gratitude,
for you are no longer of this world.

Awakening is fully available to everyone.
Never tomorrow — always now!

To sit in the truth of your own being
and not move from this place...
Now this is noble warriorship!

To feel at one with this moment is your natural state.
Use this as a direction during your meditation.

How sweet this fragrance of attending to what is!
Notice how it permeates all of life...

Paying attention to what is does not take your energy;
it shifts you from trance into wakefulness.

In meditation you become full attention,
deep relaxation, and divine revelation...all in one.

After a few moments of meditation
the rhythm of your heart
falls in step with the cosmic heart.

Once you accept that there are no accidents
all the pieces of life's puzzle fit together much easier.

On planet earth you learn the alchemy
of transforming any wound into a blessing.

Meditation is the oldest vibrational medicine.
Use it to harmonize all aspects of body, mind, and spirit.

Then this much is clear: true happiness
can only be found by turning towards the light.

Gently but firmly disconnect from your absorption with the constant mind stream of thought. Something much deeper is pulling you here. Give yourself to *that*! In this place, the form of your little self disappears and you rest in the universal Self. When thoughts or feelings arise, lovingly send them into this universal Self. Then you remain as the witness. Things come and go. You are forever fresh.

Distractions come in a multiplicity of forms.
In the center of this cyclone stand still and be the witness.
The world needs your stillness to absorb its strife.
This is the contribution you make with your daily meditation.

Meditation brings quietude and leads you
to a peace beyond all understanding.

Here you can hear the word of God.
It comes to you in the silence of your heart.

No sacrifices or suffering are needed on this path,
only a continuous surrender to what is.

Surrendering is a learning process and brings much more
than the little self could ever anticipate.

When you meditate together a sacred mandala forms and, as one of you enters into deep meditation, all the points are activated and transmission begins. This transmission is none other than your Divine Self recalling Source. Remember, Source does not belong to anyone in particular but each of you has a unique connection to it. Your way has been created specifically for you. You *are* the way. You are the alpha and the omega; the beginning and the end. You are that which never dies. Truth sits in the center of the mandala. Let it transmit through silence.

Meditation is not of this world.
It has no goal, it just is.
Just as you are...eternal, beyond form,
joyfully suspended out of time in this moment.

When there is no goal, there is no tension.
Existence pours itself into you without any friction.

Then you become the dance of the universe,
the miracle and the mystery,
the content and the container of all that is.

This is nothing new.
This has always been available.
Now it is finding its way to *you*.

Finding its way like this:
It is fresh air.
It is the bird calling in the morning.
It is awakening to what is.
It is very simple.

Take refuge in the eternal Self,
for here is the absence of desire and fear.
Here lives abundance of love and compassion.
Here lives acceptance of things as they are.
Here...all is well.

Ananda!
The bliss of deep meditation.
The wave has disappeared in the ocean.

The search is over.
You have found the secret.
Just be...
Just be...

Even the gods are bowing to you now.
Essence looks at essence and recognizes itself.

In meditation you become accustomed
to a higher vibration of love.
Over time this becomes your natural home.

Your mission here is so beautiful...
to love, to forgive, and to remember where you came from.

New frequencies are entering the earth's atmosphere right now.
Others are on this path so you can share this love.
You know who they are.

Om Shanti.
Om Shanti.
Om Shanti.

In meditation there is no grasping or attaining,
only being with what is...
celebrating the preciousness of this moment.

You are being stretched physically, emotionally and spiritually.
These are transitional times.
The old must die.
You are giving birth to the new.

Love is the guide, the teacher and your essence.

What is being stripped away from you is what is not love:
contraction, separation and the world's belief in scarcity.

You must be ready for this leap in consciousness
since you are doing it.
To be more precise: it is being done for you and through you.
You are the willing witness.
You said yes to this before you were born and took form.

Keep saying yes to what is.
It facilitates this process.

Continued meditation is the best preparation
in this time of graduation.

Your guides and teachers are taking you to the edge.
Nothing less than the great transformation is the pledge!

Love, being the essence,
is also the goal and your inevitable destiny.
It is the snake touching its own tail.
The circle is complete and perfect.

The heart is emerging.
It is for you to receive it in all its glory.

Who is meditating?
Are you aware of any effort at all?
Can you just be?

To be or not to be – that is the question, indeed.

The intellect is always moving.
The absolute is completely at rest.

Just this moment.
You are all the love contained in this moment.

Watch the tendency to move away from this moment.
Come back ever so gently.

So much turbulence in the world.
So many opposing views.
It is time to call the angels
and hold space for stillness and peace.

Offer your meditation to the world
and rise above it.
Like the lotus flower
growing through mud and water
and reaching fresh air.

Ask that a golden orb illuminates your crown.
All disturbances are pulled out of the body.
It is a fine transmutation of the gross into the subtle.

Your field is very vibrant now.
Connect again with the angels, with St.Germain, with Jesus.
Allow them to bathe you in a beautiful, liquid light.

This manna from the heavens is abundantly available.
Take of it as much as you can.

Focus on the planet now
and envelop it with rays of love and light.

Your work and willingness is greatly appreciated.
As you shower your blessings,
they come back to you a thousandfold.

Between two thoughts and two feelings there is emptiness.
Meditation is the joy of discovering these gaps.

Meditation is the quality of deep, dreamless sleep,
and being fully awake at the same time.

When you meditate the fog between you and reality dissipates.
As this happens, sense how precious you are,
how precious everyone and everything is.

When the fog is gone, there is only radiance.
See it in those you love. See it in the trees,
the plants, the rocks, the animals...

Choose a place in the world that concerns you
and put it in your heart until your heart becomes so wide
it envelopes this place. Now stay here.
Enjoy the opening of your heart...

Enjoy your service. Enjoy what you receive from it.
Keep your heart open for the rest of the day.
It is the most efficient of *all* meditations.

It is divine to pay full attention to *this* moment,
because only then is there life and celebration...

IV.
Angels and Teachers

The One manifests as the many.
Since the beginning of time many masters have come to visit here
to guide the development and evolution
of human consciousness.

As they leave the earth plane their light bodies
are even more accessible through your prayer and meditation.
It is a blessed benediction to enter into
their field of radiance.

In your lifetime the stream of Lord Buddha
and Jesus the Christ have finally merged as one.
Compassion, forgiveness, and mindfulness are now seen
as one revelation.

Your guides and teachers are drawing closer to you
on the inner planes of consciousness.
Pay attention...
When this happens, there is a beautiful softening
in the heart space.

Do not be deceived by the state of the world.
Patriarchy *is* being replaced by the compassion of the
        Divine Mother.
It is an honor to be her vessel and her testing ground.

Truth has a way of speaking for itself.
Resting in the love that you are
is your greatest contribution to world peace.

The Buddha and the Christ are emanations of this same truth,
as are you when you remember who you really are.

Go inside...See yourself...
as the eternal subject, the ever flowing source of love.

Now is the time of divine alchemy. Open the chambers of your heart and encourage the union of the sacred feminine with the sacred masculine. As they come together with respect for one another, a new era begins in your life and in the life of the planet. From the heart let this energy spread to the fingertips, the toes, and the crown. Now connect your energy with the pulse of the earth and the sound of its gentle rain and the humming of the heavenly bodies. No longer are you lost in separation. You are held in the arms of Universal Love and the whole of Creation is your home.

Take back your projections one-by-one.
What remains is you – in truth.

You are the offspring of Divine Mother and Divine Father
and eternal love unites you.
This is the glory of who you truly are.

Spread your wings...No one holds you back.
As you take flight you see the absolute in everything.

What wisdom you possess to attend to the inner life,
which leads inevitably to where Source and you are *One*!
Here is where you meet your guides and teachers.
Divine Mother sustains you and your only desire is
to share love with all that is.

You embody Life Eternal. Share this sacred gift with
everyone and everything.
Dedicate yourself to this and Spirit will stand by your side
steady and strong.

Life Eternal is revealed in your love and laughter,
in your compassion and silence.
It is who you really are. It is Divine Mother embracing you.
It is *Shiva Shakti* transforming you.
It is the victory of love over illusion.

Be thankful…
Your essence can be forgotten but it can never be taken away.
The seeds planted by the Buddha and the Christ
are finally blossoming in the hearts of many.
Whenever you gather, this perfume is released into the world.
Receive it here…now…

To be human is to care and be moved deeply by all things...
How courageous it is to be in touch with all of your feelings.

Your sensitivity is your life line to the Divine.
Be sure to make space for it, especially in meditation.

In this delicate openness, healing angels brush against you
and give you a transfusion of hope.

Your guides and teachers may use your personality
but mostly they are established in your true Self.
They are as much a part of you as you are of them.

Invite your guides and teachers to be with you.
They are luminous aspects of your true Self.
Your psychic being benefits tremendously from this exchange
and you become a doorway between dimensions.
Together you will accomplish the great work of transformation.

As the masters serve you...
so you serve others by your example.

Your guides and teachers applaud your presence,
for a planet without light workers is unlivable.

Lay down your burden, no matter what form it might take today
and travel the short journey to the present moment.
In less than a second you have arrived!

Here Christ is with a host of teachers to welcome you into
        a new consciousness.
Free of fear...free of guilt...free of oppression...
It is all so simple. Now celebrate your unity with all that is.

You are the resurrection each time you see the splendor of
        your holy self.
See *this* as your essence.

It does not matter what you believe as long as love is
        your guest of honor.
In this company you always blossom and surrender is so sweet
        it happens by itself.
Divine presence is the center and each atom of your light body
        drinks from Source.

(This message came on Good Friday)

Praying is disappearing...is sharing love...is entering into the dimension of the Divine.
Angels surround you as you pray. They are intergalactic beings at your service.

Can you relax into the perfection of this moment? Just for now do not dwell on anything else. An ease will descend upon you and the universe. You may feel the presence of your guides and teachers who love to support you exactly where you are. They are as genuine as you are and bypass the skeptical mind. They live in your devotional heart, the place that is childlike and joyful and connected to all that is.

Even the thought of your angels will invite them to light up your energy field.

Many masters and teachers are available to you at
    this moment in time.
Imagine them sitting in a circle around you.
Immediately you will feel more solid, more expansive,
    and more inspired.
Allowing their support benefits the quality of your life.

You came here to participate in the galactic event of
        transforming matter.
Some of the decisions in your life are mere reflections of
        this larger context.

It is not necessary to understand the nature of
        these promptings,
only to see the relevance of your own contribution.

You are following the call of Divine Mother.

Be bold enough to dream...Manifestation will follow!
An angel is working through each one of you...

Sense the presence of your inner teacher.
It is the wisdom part in you still connected
to the higher planes of consciousness.
It is responsible for certain life decisions
your conditioned self could never dream up.
Remember, the path is never as arduous as it looks —
only resistance makes it so.
Many teachers are walking among you now,
and you yourself are a teacher to many.
You become the angelic messenger
when you send love to a stranger.

Ramana never left his mountain.
Similarly, do not leave your place as witness.
If you still carry a single story
that says you are not good enough,
the witness will detect it and unravel it
so that you may feel your own worthiness.

Time and space have no meaning when you linger in the lap
of Divine Mother.
Her nature is such that she cares for all her children
fully and equally.

In just one instant Divine Mother unties all the knots
in your heart and you remain as pure love.
Why search any further when resting
in your true nature is all that is desired?

How comical the laws of *lila, maya,* and *samsara*!
Through divine hypnosis you strayed from Source.
Through divine grace you find your way home
to the lap of Divine Mother.

As you begin to meditate invite your guides and teachers
        to accompany you.
They reside in the etheric realms of light and love.
When they join you, you receive vision, clarity,
        and inspiration.
Ascend to these realms and be of service to the inhabitants
        of planet earth.
Service to the light is the connection link between all dimensions.

Divine Mother infuses your meditations with *supramental* light.
The crown and the heart bathe in a golden glow.
Relax into the perfection of this moment.
Do not dwell on anything else, but be available to this light
         and love.
What you taste is your unlimited power.

Know this...You are love and you are loved...
As you fully embody this experience
you change the atmosphere on this planet.

We, your guides and teachers, are very moved to be in your presence once again. In truth we never leave you, not even for a moment. We know that some of you fear that you are not able to experience us fully as of yet. Relax, then, deeply into your meditation so we may meet and merge as one.

In response to your yearning for a better world many portals of consciousness have opened. Step through them now. You are entitled to live in a reality founded in love, cooperation, and harmony. Some will laugh at you and say you are naïve, but is there any endeavor more important than surrendering to love?

Your contribution, your presence, your heart are important for this mission to succeed. We say this not to pressure you but to encourage your practice of mindfulness. All phenomena, all reactivity disappear into the silence of mindfulness. What remains is consciousness resting in itself.

Once again Divine Mother joins you
and urges you to wake up,
to walk in love...in peace...in harmony.
She blesses each and every one of you.

V.
Fear, Ego, and Acceptance

Accepting your life circumstance as a direct lesson
will bring deep relaxation and remove all resistance,
opposition, and separation to what is.
In the embrace of love, all struggles melt away.

When fear grips you in the gut, allow your belly to become soft and call upon love as your ally.

Remove all sense of victimization from your life story and you are free.

The mind has a habit of mulling over problem after problem.
Come to your centered heart and be grateful!

Do not burden yourself with a plan for some future perfection.
Right now...you are exquisite divine expression.

A willing student accepts all of life as a teacher,
especially this precious moment...
Any moment becomes precious when it is fully embraced.

Seeing your perfection does not require any effort —
Simply surrender to what is.
Simply relax into the totality of your being.
Use your quiet time to remember who you are.
One day, even in your busy time, you will no longer forget.

Your circumstances may not be easy, yet they are perfect
for now—
that is, until they change into the next invitation for you
to surrender.

Your journey will always have peaks and valleys.
Never take any of it personally.
Just advance one step from the busy mind to the silent heart
and awakening is the natural course.
Your tone is unique...
Who you are completes the celestial harmony.

As you accept gratitude as a force of grace
in your vibrational field, your ego will dissolve.

Very soon now the light will be returning.
In your heart keep the peace candle burning.
Darkness cannot be fought by itself.
Only love and light carry the hope of life.

By serving and by sharing who you are
the masters work through you
and your life takes new meaning.

Display of power is not the way of love.
Not in the time of Christ, not now.
Instead tune in to wisdom, compassion, and vision.

One messenger of light after another has been sent here.
Do not become a follower.
Become that light.

Your love is much stronger than your fear.
Otherwise, you wouldn't be here.

To live, the ego creates a case of mistaken identity. So remember this:
In the life of a seeker the ego dies a thousand deaths.
But fear not, for dismantling the ego structure is the next step
in the evolution of human consciousness.

The lower mind agonizes and doubts;
the higher mind is connected to the heart and trusts...

You will serve the most
by keeping one goal and one focus...
tapping the fullness of your inner potential.

Do not question your own contribution.
Just being an accepting presence makes a difference.

It takes time to shift old patterns,
and some simply refuse to disappear.
Do not worry yourself over this.
The golden presence of the eternal witness
lives beyond all disturbances.
Now, focus gently on the love that you are;
surely this will heal all wounds.

Let go of all pressure about having to achieve
something important.
Instead, see yourself already as achievement and perfection.
What a relief!

Accepting what is transforms what is.
Whenever you seek, you are blessed.
Whenever you find, you become the blessing.
Surrender to this...Surrender to this...

The ego mind is like a cat —
It can never be tamed but it can be witnessed.
From this great freedom arises.

The fear based mind strives for structure and security.
The heart has the courage to seek itself in the unknown.

The eternal Self knows no fear;
it does not operate out of memory.
The eternal Self is spontaneous as life itself and
is steeped in deep silence.

Listen carefully to the counsel of Spirit
and bravely step through fear after fear.
Embrace all of life with an open heart.
This is guaranteed to set you free.

Every single time you arise to the occasion
a wave of support comes your way.
One glimpse of truth and you know forever
what is real and what is not.

Since love is who you are, all you seek
is to relax and rest in yourself.
Invite the preciousness of *this* into every moment.

To fear is to forget your unshakable nature and destiny
as a light being.

To ascend does not mean to disappear.
To ascend means living in the world devoid of ego.
Such a world has openness and a presence
for good to manifest.

You are perfect as you are right now, completely and absolutely. Allow this truth to fill your heart as you feel yourself shift from doing to being, from tension to deep relaxation. Observe the subtle changes that occur when you make no effort whatsoever. You are alert...You are present...You are very open...Now, there is no you to *do* anything. In the fire of witnessing, all impurities are burned up and what remains constant is divine light. You belong to this...

Love manifests in a variety of forms. Yours is one of them.
You cannot come to rest until you have accepted
        this truth about yourself.

As you practice with this proposition,
it benefits your wellbeing immediately.
Just say to yourself:
        I am a form of love and so is my neighbor.

Over time false identifications fall by the wayside as clothes
that no longer fit and you wear the face before you were born.
Bondage is an illusion. It is the trick of a mind in confusion.
Freedom is already here and now.

The game of illusion is over. You have seen who you are:
a beautiful form of love.
One of the many—the many in the One.

Now whatever you do bears fruit. It is no longer driven by lack.
It comes out of fullness and goodness.
How lucky you are to have pierced the veil.
There is rejoicing in the heavens
        and ripples of peace all over the earth.

There is no going back. The nightmare has lost its appeal.
Your only calling is to heal.

Love has found its way home.

Stop projecting time and space.
Since only this moment is what truly exists,
you can be fully free right now!
Celebrate everything, even your misery,
and you will discover your authentic self.
Accept all that is and you become
available for right action.

Even Prince Siddhartha had to stop his search
to become the Buddha.
Why not accept your Buddha nature right now?

Trust where you came from...
Trust where you are going...
Trust who you are...
There are no mistakes, only opportunities
for you to know yourself even better.

At the core of your being there is always happiness, and it is when you stop thinking and worrying that happiness bubbles to the surface. Your life circumstances may be difficult, but to invite happiness into your heart is the choice you must make. The world of Spirit celebrates this choice. It is a choice you can make at any time. Now is a good time.

The heart is not here to close itself away from the world, but rather to open to ever increasing levels of vulnerability and sensitivity. Such a heart is also courageous and does not question why it is called here. Think of the future generations whose ancestors you are and your heart will leap with joy and nothing that is asked of you will ever be too much.

Such a vision has been held in high honor by the native peoples whose land you share. Know that Eagle and Buffalo are praying with you to revive the spirit of this land. Do not disappoint the children. They need your direction as elders. A brave heart is always willing to die by looking straight into the eye of fear.

Ask this...*Who am I?* and watch as healing takes place once the heart remembers why it has come here.

VI.
The Compassionate Heart

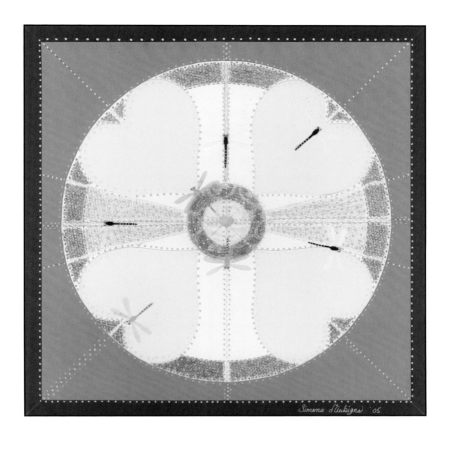

Simona d'Aubigne '05

In your open heart the world finds itself welcomed...

Listen to what the heart has to say...It speaks in parables, songs, and visions. It gives you the courage to accomplish anything you desire. Such courage comes in spite of conditioning and can be experienced in this moment. Listen...the heart never lies.

Longing for a better world is legitimate.
Be the spiritual warrior who knows no defeat
and let your heart initiate the influences
of the outer by attending the inner.
And if your heart breaks into a thousand pieces
know that each fragment shall turn into a call for compassion.
Honor this, for it is your compassion that will save the world.

Love is not blind to suffering, but it is serene
    in its compassion.
Love makes use of your presence as you make yourself
    available to love.
Listen well to those in need and you will help
    to eliminate much sorrow.

Whenever your heart softens more light becomes available
in the collective. Picture a light being in front of you, one
behind you, one to your left, and one to your right. Now
there are five of you forming a column of light and love,
a connection between earth and heaven.

As your consciousness is raised, you will see many things
in a different perspective. You will even understand how
difficulties are part of the pattern of perfection. Know that
you are being helped by so many and you, in turn, are here
to help many. Isn't this the beauty of the plan!

The blessing of one glimpse of truth allows the heart to open and is enough to propel you onto your journey...

A new consciousness is emerging simultaneously in many places all over the planet. It works through you in its own unique way. You can help each other by refraining from judgment and seeing your friend as beauty, love, and truth. This will open your own heart to its natural state of strength and vulnerability.

In service to others do not forget to serve yourself.
Only when balanced is giving also receiving.

The whole world reflects Source but only as seen through the eyes of forgiveness. Realize forgiveness does not pardon but puts on the altar a higher order of consciousness. You are the conduit of this new light; may it give meaning to *all* your choices and actions.

Think of a moment in your life when you felt very open and completely connected. Bring that memory into the present and ask to be reconnected to the depth of your being with love and silence in your heart. Now watch as you open deeply...like a beautiful flower responding to the sun.

That which sees your conditioning with compassion is
not conditioned itself.
Seeing this over and over sets you free.

All beings are blessed by the yoga of your silence.
Om Mani Peme Hung.
Om Mani Peme Hung.
Om Mani Peme Hung.

All beings are blessed by the yoga of your silence.
The jewel of the mind has reached the lotus of the heart.

True love is not blind.
It sees and transforms what it sees.

Silence is the language of the heart.
Compassion is the action of the heart.
Devotion to what *is* surrenders the heart.

You are mere presence full of compassion.
Love flows through you, and all the cells
of your body pulsate with a wonderful vibrancy.
Your heart and higher mind are in balance now.
You are no longer the thinker.
You are the current of life energy itself.
You are shifting from the personal to the *transdimensional*.
This is where you dance with your totem animals
and sit in deep meditation with your favorite saints and yogis.
Your tender heart wants to open so much more.
Soar now into the heart of the cosmos and forget your little self.
Have no fear. Let the light work for you.
Remember, you are always the observer
and your only intent is to discover more and more of who you are.
Such a blessing to be with all this light and love!
It is abundantly available, and you are worthy to receive it.

For years, even lifetimes, you have been healing yourself.
Now you are ready for the last step:
Replace all judgment with compassion,
all guilt with forgiveness, and all fear with love.
Once you have set this intention, relax and surrender to what is.
Be the observer. The observer and the observed are one.
You are one. The world is one. Consciousness is one.
Awakened are those who transcend duality
and remember oneness as the only reality.

VII.
God, Consciousness, and Silence

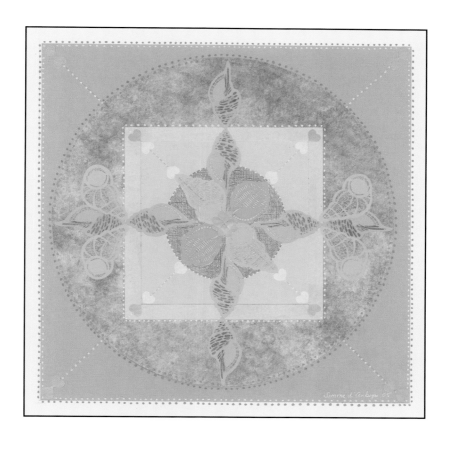

Don't forget that it is your yearning
for connection with the Divine
that facilitates its arrival.

A new consciousness is emerging within the very marrow of your bones. It is replacing compulsive thinking with silence, fear with love, and separation with union. This is humanity's silent revolution. The hidden realms oversee this process and commune with you through insight and the elevation of your vibration. More and more of you will intuit that which is true for *you* and live accordingly. Such a life displays divine design and is of service to both you and the higher plan.

The separation between God and the body
is a wound you are healing right now.
Each time you recognize who you really are
the world itself is blessed.

Whenever you share your spirit with the world,
it becomes a friendlier place.

Just for these few moments forget about the state of the world and any task you have to accomplish. Sit in the company of your spirit essence — already free, already joyful, already and always at home. Seek and find the nurturance where it is waiting for you deep inside your heart. Accept what is and resistance yields to presence, and this brings peace. Through the silence you are blessed and the world is blessed.

Likes and dislikes belong to personality and can
imprison you completely.
Falling in love with your true nature is finding God
in yourself and everyone else.

The Divine always finds a way to use you as you are today.
The lessons you are learning in your life right now
will soon become teachings to those around you.

As a body-mind eventually you dissolve,
yet as consciousness you live forever.
Take your stance as consciousness and deep peace is yours.

This peace lies beyond all understanding.
The mind cannot grasp it. The heart *already* knows it.

Let your heart be your permanent place of residence
so God can always find you at home.

Seeing oneself as source of all things is not arrogance.
It is looking through the eyes of the Divine
and finding oneself in all forms within and without.

From the very beginning until the very end,
your true nature is in charge of your journey into God.
As matter, your destiny is to fall away from here.
As light, you are eternal...

What a joy to disappear into emptiness and
to come back totally fresh!
Let silence grow on you until it has become
your most steady companion.

You are the guardian of silence and wisdom.
Realize your work is not passive,
for it brings the sacred into matter.

Your silent prayers are heard even before you utter them, and yet giving them sound brings peace to your heart.

Your authentic nature needs deep peace to replenish itself.
Silence is a wise use of your time.

When you finish a task
simply allow a little silence before the next one.
Many tasks...many silences...

Radical inner change rarely occurs overnight;
however, little transformations take place
every time you enter the silence of your being.

If thoughts still bother you, refrain from reacting to them.

Be patient...a time will come when even a storm
can no longer disturb this silence.

To abide in silence is to commune with essence.
Trials and tribulations do not exist here,
only the pulse of life renewing itself through you.

You may feel lonely and lost at sea like a little wave,
but you are the ocean, you are *all* that is.
Claim your true identity step-by-step or why not
all at once during meditation, during all of life?

Take your stance as consciousness
and immediately you feel a sense of expansion.
Worries disappear and that which is timeless comes in.
Fear is replaced with love.

Sitting quietly...without goal,
without anticipation,
without intention...something dissolves:
the wave into the ocean...
you into consciousness...

Separation is now an illusion.
In this new life you are no longer in the world.
The whole world is in you. You are home.
The climate for awakening is ideal.

Dedicate your day to truth and your actions become sacred.
Dedicate your day to silence and simplify all things.
Dedicate your heart to love and your life is divine.

Look for that in you which is unconditioned, unlimited, untouched.
See it now. It is there *now*. Seeing this sets you free.

As you can see what is true about yourself,
see it now in your brothers and your sisters.
Gone is the illusion of separation.
What remains is the beauty of creation.

Yes, it is so simple.
It is a shift of consciousness from the many to the one,
from separation to connection.
It is being intimate with all that is.

Here is the end of suffering. You have seen a glimpse of truth.
Conditioning now unravels by itself, mostly in silence.

You have graduated from the search.
From now on you are an angel of love,
aware of your human form—
resting in unity consciousness.

You are blessed to know this.
You are blessed to act upon this.
You are most blessed to be this.

What is asked of you is not complicated...
Follow your heart and you will never feel abandoned by God.

In quietude old structures of the body and the mind dissipate and disappear.

Every time you embrace the light
you have become God's messenger
and the world is a better place.

Allow your meditation time to be like a sweet caress
from Spirit that takes away stress from your body,
quieting your mind, and opening you to clarity
which *is* your true nature. You are established now
in full being-ness. No part of you is trying to run
away from the present moment. Your energy is
replenished. You are awake and you are not doing
anything. Your silence is enveloping the whole world
and touching the hearts of many. It is possible to stay
in this place throughout the day.

Beyond these words
there is a silence
that cannot be broken.
This is the true home
of the meditator.

Find your center in the silence.

You are love.
You are the consciousness
that understands these words.
You have no beginning and no end.
You are…

Allowing the longing for God is love seeking itself.

Reciting the many names of God is a useful practice...
Your name is among them.

To resonate with even one kindred spirit is enough cause for celebration.

God will never stop creating, and you shall always *be*.

Others say form is emptiness and emptiness is form.
What a lovely mystery...
You are no one and you are always the One.

At the heart of spiritual practice is this...
You are pure consciousness, even when your form is gone.

All your lifetimes you have walked towards the light.
Now — at your place of destiny — you and the light are One.

VIII.
Appeals to Humanity and Evolution

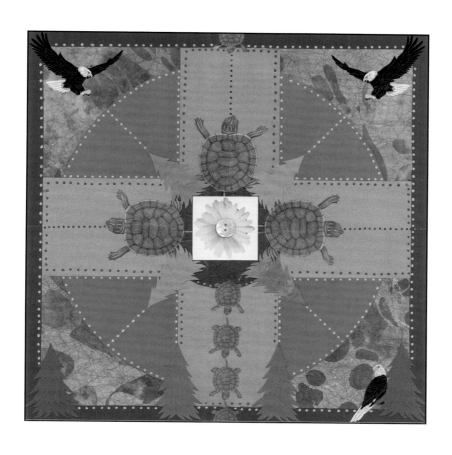

Souls incarnate in groups
and are here to learn successive lessons.

The general lesson bears repeating:
You are not the body.
You are not the mind.
You are the consciousness
that is able to perceive the body and the mind.

Often a reorientation takes place in your life
as you investigate this proposition.

For this witnessing consciousness death is not so daunting.
It is a transition, most likely an initiation,
and probably a continuation.

This time the world is learning very specific lessons:
to share resources willingly,
to listen to all points of view,
to forgive oneself and others,
and to open oneself to healing and transformation.

You have a place in this.
The members of your soul group are encouraging you,
and the choices you make touch the lives of many.

It would be senseless to repeat Atlantis.
The opening of the heart is the greatest miracle

Om Shanti.

This time you will do it.
You will overcome the weight and burden of lifetimes
and only retain what is useful.
A different future is in the making through you.

Dedication and aspiration.
Choosing, whenever you can, for the higher.
Loving the ones you meet.
Is this too much to ask?

Remember you are not alone in this task.
In meditation you can feel the invisible support.

The coming years are very critical.
The battle with the old is almost won but not quite.
Each one of you makes a difference in the balance.

Here on earth you also have a soul family supporting you.
When you gather, so do your guides and teachers.
They infuse you with a memory of all your gifts
and eager anticipation of what is yet to come.

Now is the time. This is your appointment with destiny.
Evolutionary consciousness is on the move. You are in it.
            Rejoice!

The earth lives.
The earth is sacred.
The earth is your body.

She is sending signals to you constantly.
Listen deeply so that you may resonate
in partnership with this wise one
who leads the transformation.

White Buffalo Calf Maiden is handing you the pipe.
Consider to smoke it, with respect, to purify —
to support the awakening of all beings.

May your prayers go forth in all directions
and circle the globe many times
and then come back into your own heart.

You are being asked to start afresh,
to align with your true nature.
This is not as difficult as you think.
It simply means going with the flow,
going with the times, going with evolution.

Once you say *yes*, a whole new paradigm perfectly in sync
with your willingness to show up will be activated.

Your practice of sitting together in silence bonds you deeply
with yourself, with each other, and with this earth.
All is home...All is sacred...

Like a mighty wind the Divine turns everything upside down
so a new order can emerge.
In the midst of everything shifting, there is the changelessness.
The observer in you watches and sees only perfection.

The choice for peace in one's own life
and in the collective must be made over and over.
Let it become the norm; there is no other choice.

Take a moment now to connect with sacred beings of light. They recognize and respect your essence, your integrity, and your purpose. They align you with higher vibrational dimensions, the next step in your evolution. You can enter these dimensions through meditation, prayer, shamanic journeying, dreaming, and by paying full attention to the ordinary circumstances of your daily life. Your energy field is changing ever so rapidly now. Focus on the qualities of serenity and tranquility, and simply allow the sacredness to flow...

Every time you surrender to an impulse of true love
something in the very fabric of the earth's atmosphere shifts.
Trust that each one of you carries unique gifts
perfectly suited to bring in the new paradigm.

Observing the activity of the mind moves you from the head to the heart. It invites the sacredness to descend upon you and steep you in the essence of divine love. Old habits are now too painful to maintain and new ways of being manifest. Because you came here to learn, to share, and to be of service, you are in this shift. Do not resist. In this place...

your heart is open and clear.

Only the heart can let go of the mind.
This is a great act of courage.

Beyond the strife of this tired world
that is not quite ready to die,
lies a new consciousness eager to be born.

Take a moment to connect your essence with Mother Earth
and ask her what you can do to help this planet.
As you listen to the rain, send prayers around the world
and let them shower blessings upon everyone...

As you fall deeper and deeper into meditation,
acknowledge those who sit with you:

Behind you...your ancestors...
Strong medicine women, wise shamans, and yogis.

In front of you are those of future generations.
Many have chosen planet earth fully aware of their purpose.

To your sides...your current friends and biological family,
your spiritual family and fellow travelers.

Beneath you: the vibrancy of Mother Earth.

Above you...the mighty Sky Beings,
the ascended masters,
and your guides and teachers.

And there is you yourself, holding a precious position.
You are the steward of the lineage.

Now spend some time with your totem animals.
Listen to Wolf...play with Bear...soar with Eagle...
for they are your heritage, too.

It is the time to remember which dream brought you here,
and witness, now, how you are the dreamer,
the dream, and the observer of the dream.

As your Hopi brothers are telling you:
You are the one you have been waiting for...
Your dreams are changing the world...

The evolution of consciousness
contains the strongest hope for humanity.
Your meditation is both a preparation
and collaboration for the descent
of sacred energies onto the earth plane.

Many souls are here now to assist with this shift in vibration.
Your role is to hold a steady field for them.
You will be more helpful as you dedicate
your personal inner work to benefit the collective.

As light is about to return, turn to it for sustenance.
The old *rishis* knew...The third eye center and the crown chakra
can capture the intergalactic light. Allow this...

One messenger of light after another has been sent here. Be that light! Do not become a follower, for only love and light carry the hope of life. By serving and sharing who you are, the masters work through you and your life takes new meaning. Soon the light will return. This is the season to celebrate. You are the gift! Keep the peace candle burning in your heart.

Whatever you do today, stay connected to your core...
that which is pure consciousness, which is love, which is
Eternal Self.

Right now the evolutionary impulse stimulating earth's atmosphere is creating a different form for you and through you. Cooperation in this passage is vital. In service for others you will feel, hear, and sometimes see the masters at work. In meditation they will meet you on the inner planes of consciousness. By dedicating all your efforts to the evolution of mankind you are fulfilling your purpose.

The old consciousness acts like a bully, keen on
         attacking and dividing.
Realize this old way of being is constricting in fear
and your compassion will quicken its demise.
You can alleviate unnecessary suffering
by discriminating between what is false and what is true.

This is your great opportunity to serve.
Walk your path with passion, composure, and pure intent.
This will help create a world you love to live in.
Remember, you are unique and interdependent,
and your decisions do affect the whole.
This is the beauty of your creation.

Enlightened community is a place
where each of you is a channel for spirit.
It is a place where each of you
is respected for your contribution
and for who you are.
It is a place where truth is investigated
not just one time but all the time.

Enlightened community is a place
where you challenge yourself,
where you step forward
in the full glory of who you are.
It is a place of patience and tolerance and non-judgment.

In this community nobody is lesser than.
The freedom of one person ignites that of another.
It is a model for society and helps humanity to evolve.

Your liberation is inevitable...
Do everyone a service,
start living as if it is already so.

Your silence is such a blessing.
Evolution requires it to establish a higher harmony.
You need it to discover your true self.

Perhaps you sometimes feel lost in this place,
and yet you came here to remember your Source.
Planet earth is a gathering place for many kindred spirits
        seeking awareness.
Do not despair of this density. You are only passing through.
Even in the darkest of times light workers everywhere
        never lose sight
of their aspiration to assist you along your way.

It is necessary to sit in silence
in order to help balance the chaos of the world.
Meditate on peace and see the human family as One.

Bury the sword, open your heart and speak your truth.
Your planet needs you – now!
The transformation begins with you.
Do not hesitate; give it *all* your dedication.

The invitation of the Divine is constant...
Wake up! Wake up!
Your treasure is here in front of you.
Your presence on earth is making a difference right now!

The body heals...cell by cell.
Humanity heals...person by person.
The world heals...nation by nation.

How beautiful that the kingdom of God is inside of you!
Remember, your throne is always here. Discover this
for yourself over and over in meditation. Deep silence is the key.
Gone is the little me. The search is done now,
and you are sitting in the unborn place of eternity.
Even the meditator is dissolved into Source.
You are the Source...
　　　　　now and forever.

 *Glossary*

Ananda: Hindu term for "bliss".

Avatar of the Age: A Hindu concept whereby the history of the planet is influenced by the presence of one or more very potent spiritual embodiments. They often appear when the world is in crisis.

Bodhisattva: A Buddhist term referring to a being that works out of a compassion and dedicates their own awakening to the liberation of all beings.

Divine Mother: Has been worshipped in ancient times as the sustaining force and soul of the universe. In more recent times Sweet Mother (Mirra Alfassi), Mother Meera, Ammachi, and many others have been considered as incarnations of Divine Mother.

Kuan Yin: Chinese goddess of compassion and healing.

Lila: Existence regarded as the play of the Divine.

Maya: Illusion, appearance.

Om Shanti: Peace.

Ramana: The great Indian sage Ramana Maharshi (1879-1950).

Rishis: The sages who received the Vedas, the oldest Hindu scriptures.

Samsara: Cycle of birth and death. Practical life conditioned by the laws of cause and effect.

Shiva Shakti: In the Hindu mythology Shiva, transcendent awareness, and Shakti, the compassionate energy of manifestation, are always together in mystic union.

Supramental: Level of consciousness above the mind.